Level 1 Module 4 – Let's have a part

Student Workbook

Contents

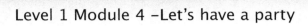

Level 1 Module 4 –Let's have a party

Contents

气球　气球　气球

蛋糕　蛋糕　蛋糕

帽子　帽子　帽子

You are going to plan a classroom party!
You will need balloons, a cake, and hats. Trace the Chinese characters.
Draw a line from the correct characters to the pictures above.

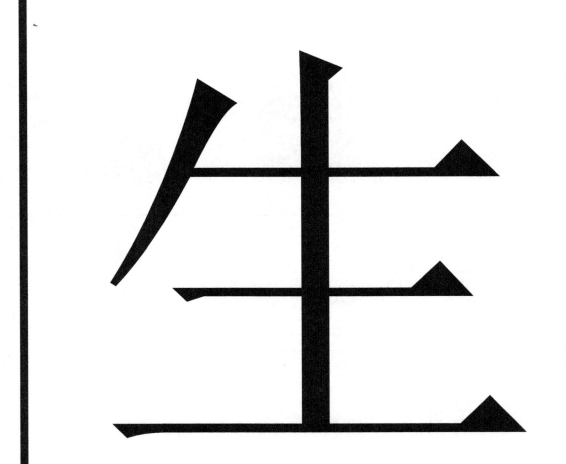

shēng

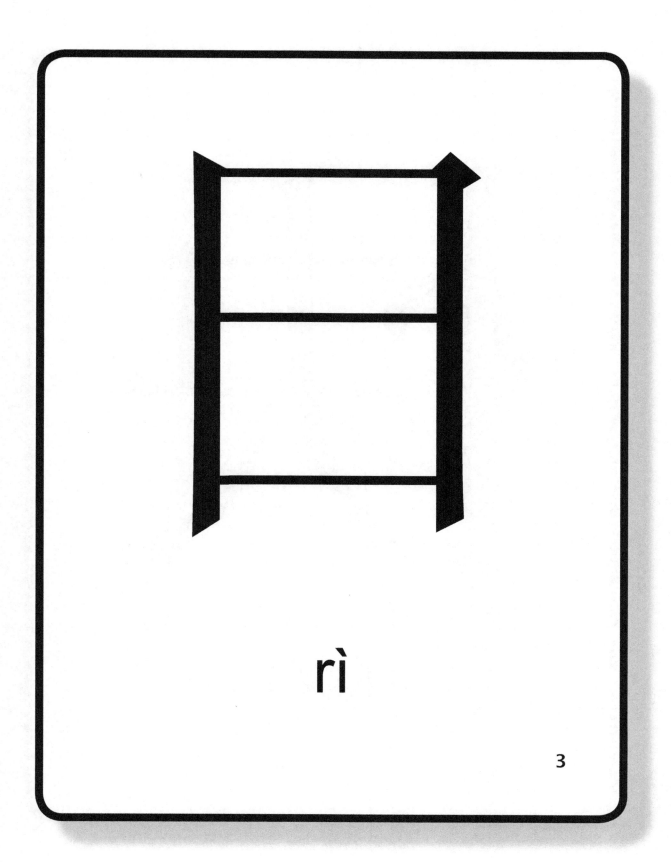

rì

3

kuài

le

Level 1 Module 4

Happy Birthday Monster!

Draw a birthday cake for Monster.

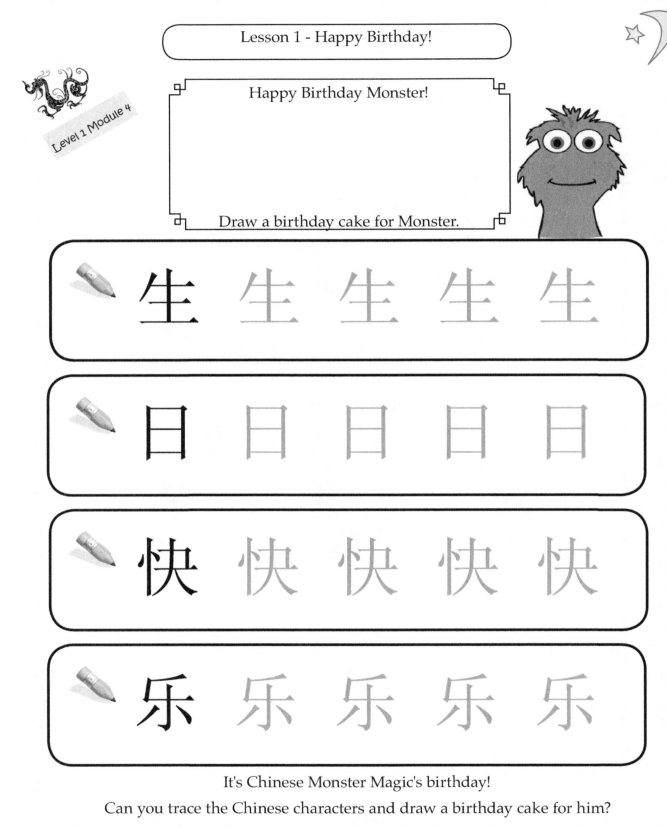

生　生　生　生　生

日　日　日　日　日

快　快　快　快　快

乐　乐　乐　乐　乐

It's Chinese Monster Magic's birthday!

Can you trace the Chinese characters and draw a birthday cake for him?

6

Level 1 Module 4

Decorate a Cake

Use your crayons to make this cake look extra special.

生日快乐

Decorate the birthday cake with lots of characters. Can you write 生日快乐 on the cake?

7

祝

zhū

nǐ

Level 1 Module 4

祝你生日快乐
祝你生日快乐
祝你生日快乐
祝你永远快乐

Sing "Happy Birthday" with a friend.

Test your friend by pointing to the Chinese characters. Trace the words to "Happy Birthday".

10

Lesson 2 - Let's make a party hat!

Level 1 Module 4

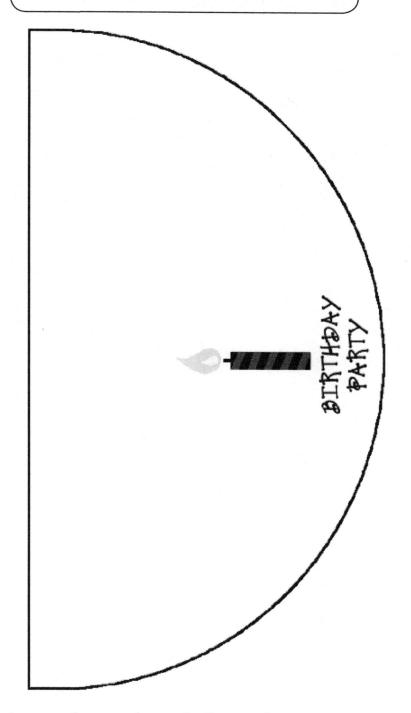

BIRTHDAY PARTY

Color and decorate the party hat with Chinese characters. Cut out and tape together to make a cone shape. Wear the party hat and tell your friends what the Chinese words mean.

11

Level 1 Module 4

NUMBERS

1	2	3	4	5	6	7	8	9	10
一	二	三	四	五	六	七	八	九	十
yi	er	san	si	wu	liu	qi	ba	jiu	shi

What's missing?

	2		4	5		7		9	
一		三		五	六		八		
	er		si	wu		qi	ba	jiu	shi

Write the characters:

一	二	三	四	五	六	七	八	九	十

Write in Characters:

7	
5	
2	
9	
3	
8	
10	
6	
1	
4	

Write 1-10 in Chinese!

Can you fill in the missing numbers?

When you have completed the worksheet, test a friend!

Level 1 Module 4

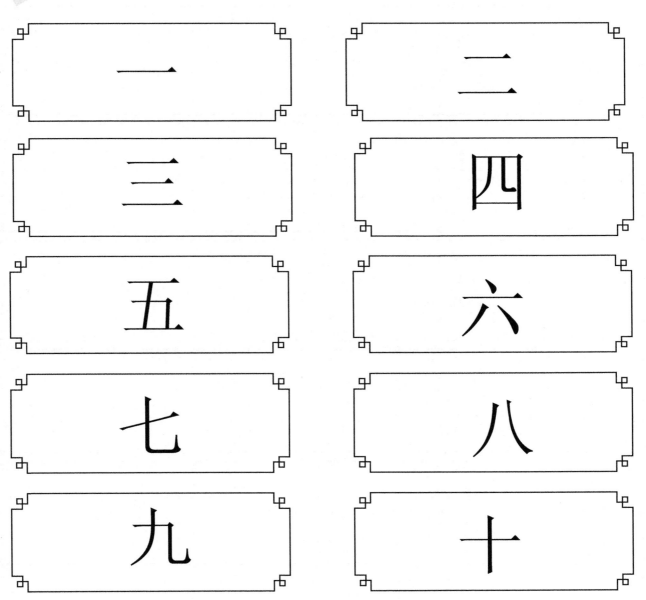

一

二

三

四

五

六

七

八

九

十

Have lots of fun playing games with the Number flash cards. Draw objects on the cards to match the Chinese character. Cut out each mini flashcard and play matching games with your friend.

Level 1 Module 4

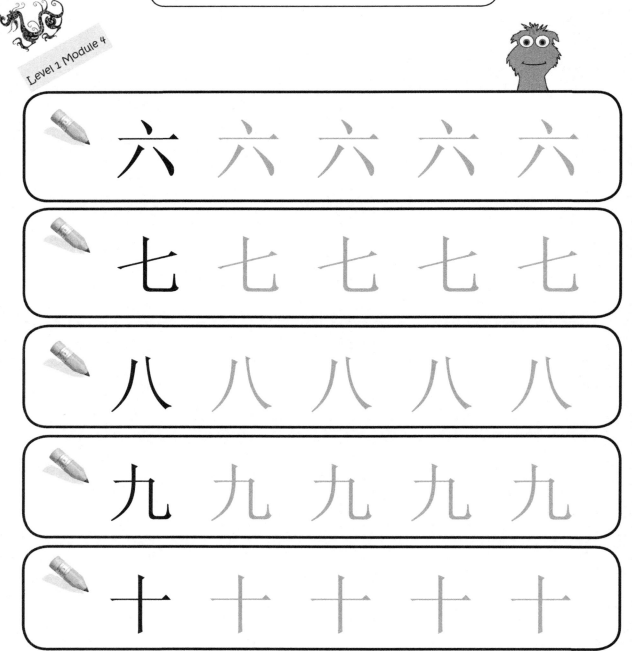

六　六　六　六　六

七　七　七　七　七

八　八　八　八　八

九　九　九　九　九

十　十　十　十　十

It's Chinese Monster Magic's birthday!

Can you trace the Chinese characters and draw a birthday cake for him?

14

一二三四五六七

我的朋友在哪里?

在哪里?

在哪里?

我的朋友在哪里?

Rehearse the "Where's my friend" rhyme and say it to the teacher.

Level 1 Module 4

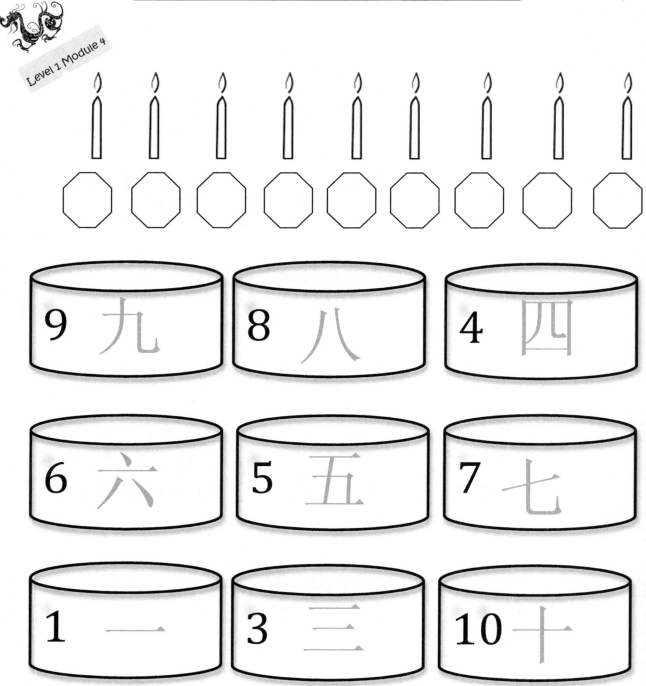

9 九

8 八

4 四

6 六

5 五

7 七

1 一

3 三

10 十

Read the number on the cake and draw the correct number of candles on each cake. Trace the Chinese character.

Level 1 Module 4

祝你生日快乐

Let's make a birthday card.

Write the Chinese characters for "Happy Birthday" and decorate the card for a family member or a friend.

红　蓝　黄　绿

red　　　blue　　　yellow　　　green

红 红 红 红 红

蓝 蓝 蓝 蓝 蓝

黄 黄 黄 黄 黄

绿 绿 绿 绿 绿

A good way of remembering the meaning of Chinese characters is to see pictures inside them. Use your imagination and draw a picture inside each character.

Trace the characters all by yourself.

18

hóng

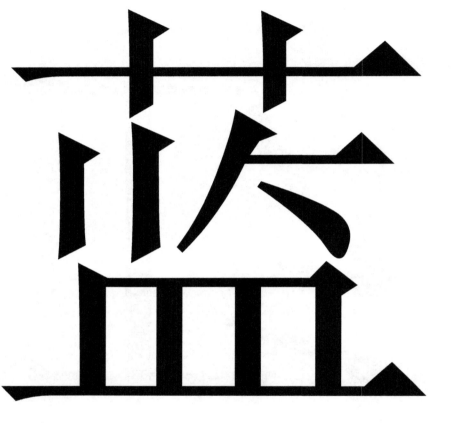

lán

huáng

21

lù

黄　绿

红　蓝

Listen to your teacher. Color the balloons and match the Chinese characters to the correct balloons.

Level 1 Module 4

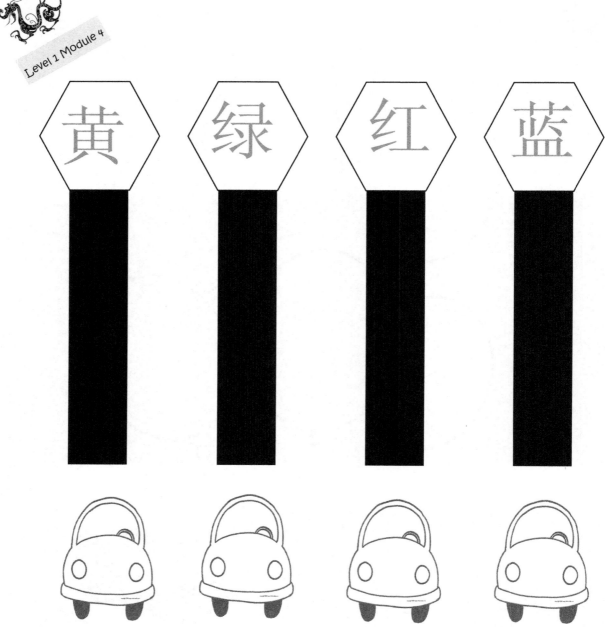

黄　绿　红　蓝

Color and cut out the signs and cars.

With a friend play the "Start your car" game.

24

Level 1 Module 4

黄	绿
红	蓝

You will make a page for a class book. Look at each Chinese character and draw an object to match the color. Your teacher will collect all the pages and staple them together. Have fun reading the Chinese color book!

25

Level 1 Module 4

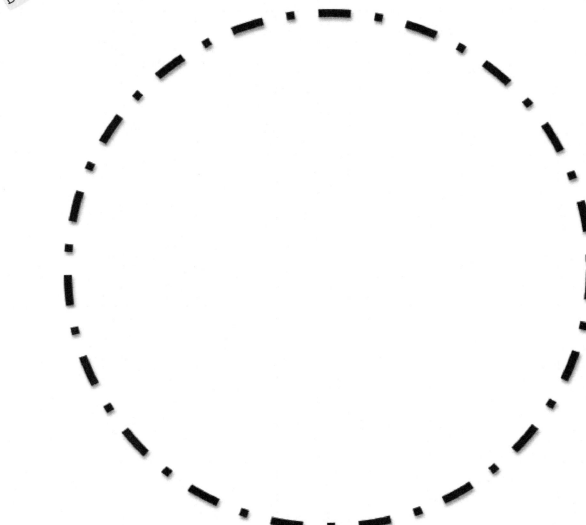

Listen to your teacher. When you hear a food in Chinese, draw and color the food on your plate.

这是什么?

Listen to your teacher. When you hear a food in Chinese, color the correct food.
Say the foods in Chinese to a friend.

27

Level 1 Module 4

好吃　　　不好吃

Use these "tastes good" and "tastes bad" faces when you have a taste test with your class. Trace the Chinese characters and cut out carefully.

28

好吃　好吃　好吃

好吃　好吃　好吃

不好吃　不好吃

不好吃　不好吃

Trace the Chinese characters for "tastes good" and "tastes bad".

Level 1 Module 4

😊 好吃	☹ 不好吃

You have will have a taste test today and try different foods!

When you or your friend tastes the food, draw the food in either the 好吃 or the 不好吃 section. Tell your friend in Chinese which foods you like the most.

生 日 快 乐

Happy Birthday

You will draw a party picture.

Listen to your teacher and draw the objects you hear in Chinese. Make your party colorful and lots of fun!

Level 1 Module 4

We are having a Party!

Dear Parents,

During Chinese lessons this month, we have been learning new words related to our theme – "Let's have a Party".

We are having a classroom party on

_____

Each student in the class is asked to bring some food to share at our Chinese party. (fruit and simple food is encouraged)

We will be speaking Chinese and practicing all the new words we have learned this month.

Thank you,

_____

生日快乐

Take this letter home to your parents.

In the next Chinese lesson you will be able to use all the new Chinese words during a class party!

Level 1 Module 4

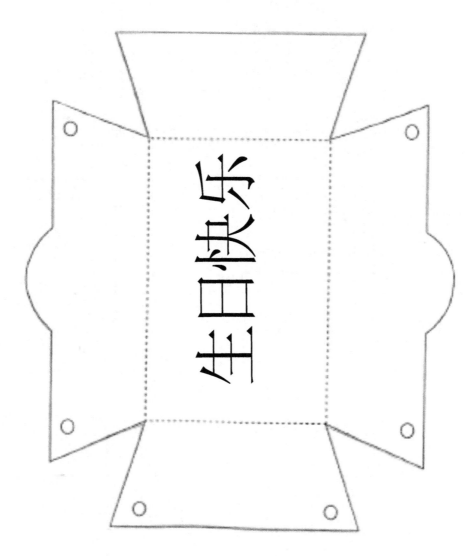

You will make a gift for a friend. Decorate the box with as many Chinese characters as you can write! Cut out carefully and tape together. Your teacher will give you candy to put inside the box.

Don't forget to say 谢谢 when you receive your gift at the class party!

33

Level 1 Module 4

Date: _____

To the parents / caregivers of

_____

Your child has just completed a Chinese Module –Let's have a party!

The best thing about learning Chinese is:

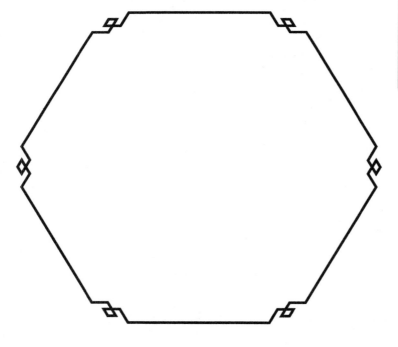

Student signature: _____

Parent signature: _____

Writing

I can:

• Write Happy Birthday using Chinese characters
• Write Numbers 1–10
• Make a Birthday Card using Chinese words
• Write characters for tastes good and tastes not good

Oral Interaction

I can:

• Sing Happy Birthday in Chinese
• Say rhyme – Where's my Friend?
• Say rhyme – Red Balloon
• Respond to How old are you?
• Describe color of balloons
• Identify simple food
• Count objects 1–10

Reading

I can:

• Read a Happy Birthday banner
• Recognize colors – red, green, blue and yellow
• Recognize Chinese characters for fruit / food
• Play a game called – Teacher says

34

Printed in Great Britain
by Amazon

22328667R00024